TExES

Principal as Instructional Leader
Practice Questions

TExES Practice Tests and Exam Review for the
Texas Examinations of Educator Standards

DEAR FUTURE EXAM SUCCESS STORY

First of all, **THANK YOU** for purchasing Mometrix study materials!

Second, congratulations! You are one of the few determined test-takers who are committed to doing whatever it takes to excel on your exam. **You have come to the right place.** We developed these practice tests with one goal in mind: to deliver you the best possible approximation of the questions you will see on test day.

Standardized testing is one of the biggest obstacles on your road to success, which only increases the importance of doing well in the high-pressure, high-stakes environment of test day. Your results on this test could have a significant impact on your future, and these practice tests will give you the repetitions you need to build your familiarity and confidence with the test content and format to help you achieve your full potential on test day.

Your success is our success

We would love to hear from you! If you would like to share the story of your exam success or if you have any questions or comments in regard to our products, please contact us at **800-673-8175** or **support@mometrix.com**.

Thanks again for your business and we wish you continued success!

Sincerely,
The Mometrix Test Preparation Team

TABLE OF CONTENTS

Practice Test #1

Selected Response

1. A principal has received notice that the current standards will be phased out and a new set of standards will be adopted for the upcoming school year. Which of the following actions should the principal take first regarding curriculum development and revision?

  a. Set aside money in the school budget for purchasing new curriculum.
  b. Create a committee to advise the principal on curriculum adoption.
  c. Plan dates for training teachers about the new curriculum.
  d. Identify what standards are changing and how the current curriculum and resources align to the new standards.

2. School leaders can organize teachers into data inquiry teams to identify and address student academic needs. What accurately describes something school leaders should direct these teams to do?

  a. Develop action plans according to data analyses.
  b. Support the implementation of the action plans.
  c. Analyze data from summative assessments only.
  d. Analyze data by classes, not individual students.

3. Which of the following best represents a mutually beneficial relationship between a school and a community organization?

  a. A neighborhood grocery store donates bottled water to the basketball team for home games.
  b. The school hosts a clothing drive for a local homeless shelter once a year.
  c. A local church has permission to use the school library for meetings on Saturday mornings and the principal is permitted to make announcements to the attendees during the meetings.
  d. A medical clinic near the school offers free immunizations and physicals to students actively enrolled at the school.

4. Which of the following most correctly represents criteria requiring a school to hold a Manifestation Determination Review for a student who receives special education services?

  a. The school seeks a discipline-related placement change for more than 10 days in a row.
  b. The school suspends a student on a one-time basis for more than 10 consecutive days.
  c. The school has expelled or otherwise excluded a student for discipline-related reasons.
  d. The school requests the parents to attend this meeting following a disciplinary incident.

5. What is most true about effective new teacher induction programs?

  a. They should focus on supporting new teachers but not leaders.
  b. They should give only new teachers professional development.
  c. They should use self-assessments and reflection for teachers to measure performance.
  d. They should improve student achievement via teacher efficacy.

1

6. Which of the following is true regarding best practices for school leaders when giving teachers observational feedback?

    a. Leaders should give feedback statements rather than asking questions.
    b. Leaders should disregard strengths to focus on improving weaknesses.
    c. Leaders should emphasize all identified areas for improvement equally.
    d. Leaders should include some specific next steps attainable for teachers.

7. Which of the following statements correctly reflects considerations for school leaders in supporting school improvement through effective resource management?

    a. The school vision and goals are most dependent upon physical resources.
    b. Material resources are priority as they are needed for a safe, comfortable teaching and learning environment.
    c. Managing fiscal resources is necessary for managing other resources, with some exceptions.
    d. Managing human resources is necessary for smaller class sizes and optimal student learning and achievement.

8. What is the primary reason that curriculum and instruction must be aligned to assessment?

    a. School leaders must be able to justify why they select curriculum and resources.
    b. Teachers must know what to teach in the classroom.
    c. Assessments that are not aligned with curriculum and instruction will not accurately measure what students learned.
    d. Alignment of curriculum and assessments makes it easier to analyze and compare student performance data.

9. A school leader would like to increase the use of differentiated instruction as an instructional strategy on campus. Which of the following actions would be most effective in achieving this goal?

    a. Publicly recognize teachers who use differentiated instruction in the classroom.
    b. Purchase books about differentiated instruction and distribute them to all of the teachers.
    c. Model differentiated instruction during professional development sessions and monitor classroom implementation.
    d. Hire an instructional coach that can train teachers how to use differentiated instruction in the classroom and evaluate their efficacy.

10. Which of the following is true about the efficacy of new teacher induction programs on schools?

    a. They make new teachers more comfortable, not more effective.
    b. They increase the rates at which the new teachers are retained.
    c. They enhance teacher instructional skills, not teacher leadership.
    d. They help education inequities more than student achievement.

11. Other than classroom observations, which of the following would best provide an additional source of data for teacher evaluation?

    a. Student performance data.
    b. Student surveys.
    c. Parent surveys.
    d. Teacher self-assessments.

12. Which of the following represents a principle informing school leader support and professional development (PD) of teachers throughout their careers?

    a. PD must be continuing and supported by repetition and follow-up to change teaching over time.

    b. PD for teachers should be focused on practice and not on theoretical bases.

    c. PD is best administered as a stand-alone process within individual schools.

    d. When school leaders furnish PD, they should be sure to include the newest, most popular topics.

13. Which of the following statements does not support standardized classroom practices and procedures?

    a. Improving the cost-efficiency of school programs by reducing differentiation.

    b. Increasing the conformity to curricula within departments.

    c. Promoting safety throughout the school.

    d. Ensuring that students can expect the same teaching style from each teacher.

14. A school leader is monitoring the curricular programs to determine whether student needs are being met. Which of the following would provide the most valid indication that the curricular programs are meeting student needs?

    a. Assessment data shows that students are meeting minimum performance standards.

    b. Parent survey data demonstrates that parents are pleased with the curricular programs.

    c. Teacher observations are positive, overall.

    d. Assessment data shows that most students are demonstrating academic growth.

15. At a PTA meeting, a concerned community member stated that there were no programs offered at the high school that prepared students for jobs in the community and that there was too much focus on sending students to college. Which of the following best describes the action that the principal can take to address the community member's concern?

    a. Inform the community member that preparing students for college is the school's primary responsibility.

    b. Promise the community member that course offerings will be revised for the upcoming school year.

    c. Ask the community member which jobs in the community the school should prepare students for.

    d. Collect and review employment trend data in the community to determine if school course offerings need to be revised to meet community needs.

16. The Dean of Instruction of a 9th grade high school academy would like to monitor student progress for the grading period. Which of the following sources of data would best inform the dean of student progress?

    a. Student portfolios of work samples from previous and current marking periods.

    b. Benchmark scores from the previous and current marking periods.

    c. Anecdotal teacher notes.

    d. Report card grades for the marking period.

17. What have researchers found regarding the relationship between student academic self-concepts and student outcomes?

   a. Students' academic self-concepts are correlated with their succeeding later in life.
   b. Students' academic self-concepts are correlated with their academic achievement.
   c. Students' academic self-concepts are correlated with socioeconomic status more than home settings.
   d. Students' academic self-concepts are correlated with enrollment in smaller schools.

18. Compared to majority rule and committees, what is a more salient characteristic of group consensus as a way of making collaborative educational decisions?

   a. It is more time-efficient than these other methods.
   b. It can undermine commitment for minority voters.
   c. It is more thorough and hears all members' voices.
   d. It may make member time and effort not worth it.

19. Among professional development learning opportunities that school leaders can incorporate into daily teacher activities, which is/are collaborative?

   a. Conducting action research.
   b. Reflection during practice.
   c. Reading current research.
   d. Structured observations.

20. The school principal institutes a professional learning community made up of social studies and reading teachers from grades 6th through 8th. This professional learning community is an example of which of the following?

   a. Horizontal alignment of curriculum and instruction.
   b. Vertical alignment of curriculum and instruction.
   c. Horizontal and vertical alignment of curriculum and instruction.
   d. Cross-cultural integration of curriculum and instruction.

21. A principal notices that even though teachers actively participate in professional development throughout the school year, there seems to be little evidence of changes in instructional practices on campus. Which of the following questions best addresses the concern of the principal?

   a. What is the process for giving feedback on the efficacy of professional development offered to teachers?
   b. Are professional development sessions aligned to the curriculum, instruction, and programs of this campus?
   c. How much does professional development impact the school budget?
   d. How can I make time in my schedule to attend professional development sessions with the teachers?

22. A principal is planning for the upcoming school year. Which of the following factors would most directly impact student learning?

   a. The number of math and reading teachers on staff and the size of the classes that they teach
   b. The benchmark testing schedule for the academic year
   c. The time that school starts each day
   d. The number of computers purchased

4

23. A school principal would like to develop a positive partnership with the school community. Which of the following actions would best help the principal to achieve this goal?

   a. Publish a monthly school newsletter with reminders for important school events.
   b. Host a student award ceremony each semester to highlight school and student successes.
   c. Attend all school athletic events.
   d. Send a survey to all community members to get their feedback on school performance.

24. Which kind of data best helps teachers to identify strengths and needs in their teaching practices, support capacity-building, and identify specific remedial student groups?

   a. Formative data
   b. Summative data
   c. Student profiles
   d. Enrollment data

25. How can school leaders best promote openness and collaborative decisions in ethical school leadership and make ethical conversation integral to their school culture?

   a. They can analyze the ethical implications of any decision for the school community.
   b. They can maintain constancy in their ethical frameworks throughout their careers.
   c. They can accept needed funding even if the donors require less effective methods.
   d. They can regularly initiate discussions for self-examination and ethics development.

26. A Dean of Instruction of a middle school wants to increase the number and variety of resources that teachers have access to. Which of the following actions should the dean take to accomplish this goal?

   a. Encourage teachers to purchase instructional resources and provide reimbursement for their expenses.
   b. Survey teachers to identify which resources they would like to have and purchase resources from their suggestions.
   c. Provide teachers with asynchronous, on-demand professional development sessions online.
   d. Seek free and discounted resources from vendors in the local area.

27. Which of the following represents the primary source of school funding?

   a. Allotments from the federal government
   b. Grants
   c. Donations
   d. Property taxes

28. Which of the following actions taken by a principal best addresses the problem of having primarily novice teachers on staff?

   a. Increased teacher observations and feedback
   b. Facilitating collaborative teaching and team teaching
   c. Monitoring data closely
   d. Providing tutorials for students after school

29. Which of the following pieces of information would be most relevant when determining how to differentiate instruction for students?

a. Previous academic performance, special needs (such as a physical or learning disability), and learning style
b. Previous academic performance, demographics, and socioeconomic status
c. Student interests, career goals, and grade point average
d. Student interests, parental input, and learning style

30. Which of the following would be most likely to cause an administrator to look for outside resources in assisting students and their families?

a. A student is having difficulty in math class.
b. Two students participated in a physical altercation.
c. A student and their family are struggling financially and are in need of food and clothing.
d. A student will be the first in the family to graduate high school.

31. Which of the following practices best represents the least restrictive environment (LRE) for a student who receives special education services?

a. The student remains in a classroom with other students who receive special education services throughout the day, with the exception of ancillary classes.
b. The student attends classes with students who do not receive special education services, but reports to a special education teacher's classroom during independent practice of each core class.
c. The student reports to a special education teacher's classroom for math and reading only.
d. The student attends classes with students who do not receive special education services and classroom teachers provide modifications to the curriculum and/or accommodations to assist the student.

32. In terms of assessment, which of the following is a true statement that school leaders should consider when minimizing bias and maximizing equity for all students?

a. Accommodations given to students during testing are inherently unfair.
b. Progress monitoring using student data decreases achievement gaps.
c. Achievement gaps can be resolved by testing low performing students frequently and extensively.
d. Assessment validity and reliability nullifies most non-standardized test results.

33. Experts advise school leaders to create a clear vision for the best use of school-wide student achievement data and to communicate this vision. What else do they recommend for using these data?

a. School leaders should institute supports to develop a data-driven school culture.
b. School leaders should instruct faculty, not students, to understand and use data.
c. School leaders should develop and maintain data systems specific to the school.
d. School leaders should separate data from the cycle of continuous improvement.

34. In reference to the Supportive School Discipline Initiative (SSDI), former US Attorney General Eric Holder said a federal initiative to guide school disciplinary practices would "make schools safe, supportive and inclusive for all students" and would "keep America's young people safe and on the right path." How did he say it would do these things?

a. By making discipline less exclusionary.
b. By divorcing discipline from civil rights.
c. By getting data from resource officers.
d. By referring discipline to peace officers.

35. During the annual summer meeting, the math department chair expresses concern that the math teachers do not have enough collaborative time to plan lessons and discuss student performance. Which of the following solutions would best address the department chair's concern?

a. Make adjustments to the master schedule to allot collaborative planning time for the math department.
b. Offer extra duty pay for math teachers to stay after school and plan together.
c. Purchase a technology platform that will allow the teachers to communicate asynchronously online.
d. Place substitute teachers in the math classrooms monthly to allow teachers time to plan together.

36. Under the National Education Association (NEA) Code of Ethics, Principle I, Commitment to the Student, educators are enjoined against doing a number of things, including that they: "[s]hall not disclose information about students obtained in the course of professional service unless disclosure serves a compelling professional purpose or is required by law." This reflects which of the following federal laws?

a. The Civil Rights Act of 1964
b. The Family Educational Rights and Privacy Act (FERPA) and/or the Individuals with Disabilities Act (IDEA)
c. Americans with Disabilities Act (ADA) Amendments Act Title II
d. Rehabilitation Act Section 504

37. To build a positive culture of learning and high expectations, school leaders can guide teachers to identify instructional activities that are aligned to the curriculum and have been proven to be effective. Which of the following is an indicator of effective implementation of instructional activities?

a. Differentiated instruction.
b. Increased student attendance.
c. Flexible student grouping.
d. Focused discussions and effective interaction between students.

38. A school leader has decided to hire an instructional coach to support the teachers' growth. Which of the following is the most likely result of this decision?

    a. The instructional coach will help the leadership team supervise and evaluate teachers.

    b. The instructional coach will make the decisions regarding professional development and training on campus.

    c. Having an instructional coach will eliminate the need for professional development and training on campus.

    d. The instructional coach will provide individualized, targeted support to teachers to help them to grow.

39. Which of the following statements is most accurate about how school leaders align school policies and practices with federal, state, district, and local school system policies?

    a. State standardized assessment instruments are based solely on standards developed by states.

    b. Individual schools directly apply state standards for developing their standardized assessments.

    c. Schools directly reflect system standards, and yet ultimately are also aligned with federal policy.

    d. Local school districts develop standardized assessments applying the federal standards directly.

40. Which of the following sources and types of data would be best to use to provide feedback to teachers so that they can improve student learning?

    a. Classroom observations, student class grades, and summative assessment data.

    b. Formative assessment data, attendance data, and behavior data.

    c. Classroom observations, survey data, and diagnostic testing data.

    d. Formative assessment data, diagnostic testing data, and projected performance data.

41. Which of the following is most effective in motivating members of the educational community when implementing new policies?

    a. Delegating authority to staff members.

    b. Communicating unexpected barriers to the community as they arise.

    c. Sharing the policies frequently using a variety of communication channels.

    d. Including stakeholders in the development of new policies.

42. To gather feedback from key stakeholders about the relationship between their opinions about the significance of education and the school's vision and goals, which of these should a school leader do?

    a. Develop a series of critical questions appropriate to this topic.

    b. Develop a few open-ended questions to stimulate discussions.

    c. Develop a school task force to interview all of the stakeholders.

    d. Develop a series of meetings wherein stakeholders discuss this.

43. According to research related to the factors that contribute to the success of higher-performing public schools, which of the following is true?

 a. The school leader is the single defining success factor
 b. School success is based on a complex set of interrelated factors
 c. Schools cannot be successful without additional funding
 d. Factors related to curriculum and instruction are the most important determinants of success

44. A high school principal is concerned that ninth grade students who read below grade level are not performing well on benchmark tests in Reading and Writing. Which of the following steps should the principal take to best address this concern?

 a. Provide test preparation sessions for these students after school and on weekends and monitor student attendance to the sessions.
 b. Integrate reading and writing skills into all subject areas and provide training to all teachers on fundamental reading strategies.
 c. Increase the opportunities that students have to spend in the school library.
 d. Purchase a reading software program that students can use at home.

45. Which of the following should NOT be considered when a school principal observes teachers in their classrooms?

 a. The quality and rigor of assignments given to students.
 b. The implementation of strategies learned in professional development sessions.
 c. Classroom environment and culture.
 d. The teacher's tenure or contract status.

46. Which of the following is an effective way to use community resources to support student learning?

 a. Invite local churches to host a back-to-school drive to provide students with school supplies.
 b. Partner with local businesses to provide free tutoring to students after school.
 c. Partner with local businesses to host field trips for students.
 d. Invite local businesspersons in the community to mentor students.

47. Which of the following would most impact the success of a new teacher induction program?

 a. Providing optional coaching sessions for new teachers.
 b. Assigning mentors to new teachers based on the seniority of the mentor teacher.
 c. Providing opportunities for collaboration and leadership development.
 d. The school leader facilitates all aspects of the induction program.

48. Who typically makes student enrollment projections for determining school budgets?

 a. District Offices of Achievement and Accountability alone project the student enrollments.
 b. District Offices of Achievement and Accountability with school leader revision as needed.
 c. The school leader alone projects the student enrollments for his or her school every year.
 d. Final projections are by committees from the district finance and student support offices.

49. A teacher complains to the principal that the feedback from their most recent evaluation was not fair because it did not provide a well-rounded view of their performance. Which of the following is the best action that the principal can take to address this concern?

    a. Conduct additional observations of the teacher at various days of the week, times of the day, and in varied circumstances.

    b. Explain why the evaluation was accurate.

    c. Find other staff members who can confirm what was written in the teacher's evaluation.

    d. Show the teacher that all protocols and policies were followed in conducting the evaluation.

50. When selecting professional development for staff, which of the following should a leader consider first?

    a. The cost of the professional development

    b. Whether the professional development has been effective on other campuses

    c. The areas of deficit of staff based on observations and evaluations

    d. The alignment of the professional development with the campus vision and goals

51. The school principal reviews classroom observation and feedback with assistant principals weekly, but often has very few classroom observations of their own conducted in preparation for the weekly meeting. What action should the school principal take to increase the frequency of classroom visits?

    a. Make a commitment to visit classrooms every morning before the day gets too busy.

    b. Clear their schedule on a specific day of the week to dedicate to classroom visits.

    c. Plan out the classrooms that should be visited for the week and add them to the calendar with reminders.

    d. Carry classroom observation forms at all times and visit classrooms when an opportunity presents itself.

52. The math department is excited that for the third consecutive time, most of the seventh-grade students have earned perfect scores on their six-week report cards. The Dean of Instruction is concerned by this news and requests to examine student work samples and class grades. Which of the following is a likely reason that the dean is concerned?

    a. The data may indicate that the students are not receiving rigorous curriculum and instruction.

    b. The math department's performance may have misinterpreted the student data.

    c. The few students who did not receive perfect grades may be falling behind.

    d. The students are likely committing acts of academic dishonesty.

53. What do psychologists recommend regarding tiered models of student behavior management in education?

    a. Tiered models of behavior management work only with school-wide behavior support systems.

    b. Tiered models of behavior management are most effective when addressing individual disruptive student behavior.

    c. Tiered models of behavior management are most applicable for classroom or school-wide implementation.

    d. Tiered models of behavior management are judged best for individuals, classrooms, or schools.

54. On which of the following do the Individuals with Disabilities Education Act and the Family Education Rights and Privacy Act differ with respect to student records?

a. Requiring instruction and training of educators on records confidentiality
b. Defining which student records are considered to be educational records
c. Determining conditions for destroying educational records via state laws
d. Regulating records collection, maintenance, confidentiality, or disclosure

55. An elementary school principal serves at a school in which many of the parents of students speak little or no English. The language barrier creates challenges in communication, parent engagement, and the reinforcement of learning at home. Which of the following actions would best help the principal to address this challenge?

a. Hire a translator to communicate with parents.
b. Partner with an adult ESL program in the community and offer free ESL classes on campus.
c. Translate all school documents to the languages of the parents.
d. Ask students to translate information for their parents.

56. A school leader requests that teachers identify exemplary student work in PLCs and post the student work in their classrooms. The school leader regularly visits classrooms to view and evaluate the work that is posted. Which of the following best explains why the school leader made this request?

a. The school leader desires to be involved in analyzing student work.
b. The school leader is encouraging teacher collaboration.
c. The school leader is enforcing adherence to the standards-based curriculum.
d. The school leader believes that all students should be recognized for their performance.

57. Which of these is recommended for school leaders to plan classroom visits effectively for giving teachers useful observational feedback?

a. Completing a checklist during every classroom visit
b. Giving teachers individual, not collective, feedback
c. Making walk-throughs to give summative feedback
d. Using statistics to give individual teacher feedback

58. Which of the following accurately represents how school leaders can promote equitable access to curriculum for all students and their parents?

a. They can make staff more comfortable in discussing diversity without promoting equity.
b. They can clarify school staff misconceptions related to deficit theories about minorities.
c. They can model equity in daily interactions, but should avoid confronting discrimination.
d. They can create safe environments, though student support networks are not their job.

59. Which of the following best describes rigorous instruction?

a. Rigor in academic instruction refers to curriculum and instruction that is challenging to students.
b. Rigor in academic instruction refers to honors, advanced placement, and dual credit courses.
c. Rigor in academic instruction refers to appropriate grading and feedback on student work.
d. Rigor in academic instruction refers to teaching above student grade levels.

60. Which of the following should school principals primarily look for when observing teachers in classrooms for evaluation purposes?

a. They should focus on what students want to learn rather than what they want them to learn.

b. They should look for how comfortable the teacher is with the lesson content and method of delivery.

c. They should look for evidence of learning such as student responses to checks for understanding and student work products.

d. They should focus on physical classroom setup.

61. Which of the following statements is true about a school climate in which students feel supported?

a. Students find resources and support are readily available to them.

b. Students who share multiple classes are more likely to form relationships with one another.

c. Student roles and responsibilities are clearly defined in policy handbooks.

d. Student feelings of support are not affected by interactions with adults.

62. What does research show about school leaders distributing leadership responsibilities for implementing a school vision and goals?

a. The most effective leaders are found to influence student achievement and school efficacy directly.

b. Today's schools cannot be led by one principal without significant participation by other educators.

c. The traditional model of single, formal leadership exists because teachers lack a principal's expertise.

d. Educational programs developed by one principal are easier for principals who follow to maintain.

63. What is the primary benefit of conducting teacher evaluations?

a. Evaluations can provide feedback to staff members so that they can grow professionally.

b. Evaluations are needed to determine who is not performing to expectations.

c. Evaluations can help identify the professional development and coaching that teachers need.

d. Evaluations can be used to remove an underperforming teacher from their position.

64. What is the primary purpose of professional learning communities?

a. To hold teachers accountable

b. To make it easier to monitor teaching and learning

c. To facilitate collaboration among teachers

d. To set and achieve instructional goals

65. Which of the following actions best exemplifies a focus on school-wide rigorous curriculum and standards-based instruction?

a. Increase the number of advanced placement and dual credit courses offered on the master schedule.

b. Increase the number of students taking college entrance exams.

c. Evaluate campus based assessments for alignment to the standards and curriculum and revise where appropriate.

d. Offer after-school tutorials for students who are falling behind.

66. Which of the following best describes the relationship between the school principal and the school board?

 a. The school principal recommends the hiring and termination of teachers to the school board.
 b. The school principal reports campus data to the school board at board meetings.
 c. The school board hires and supervises the superintendent, who in turns hires and supervises the school principal.
 d. The school board implements state and local policies that the principal must abide by.

67. The fine arts teacher would like to construct a mural outside of the art building. The school leader believes it is a good idea, but does not have the funds to purchase the supplies required to complete the mural. What recommendation should the school leader make to the art teacher?

 a. Host a fundraiser to obtain money to purchase supplies.
 b. Ask the Athletic Director to use money from the athletics fund.
 c. Charge art students an art fee to obtain money for the mural.
 d. The art teacher cannot construct the mural this school year.

68. Which of the following is a primary benefit of professional learning communities?

 a. To provide opportunities for teachers to share ideas.
 b. To provide constructive feedback on student performance.
 c. To identify areas in the curriculum that need revision.
 d. To ensure that the standards-based curriculum is delivered.

69. What is the MOST accurate description among ways that effective school leaders openly share data with students and staff?

 a. Involving identified students for developing data systems
 b. Involving designated staff in developing assessment plans
 c. Involving students in knowing and tracking their own data
 d. Involving overall school data as the basis for student goals

70. A school leader wants to enlist support for change on campus. Which of the following actions should be taken first?

 a. Communicate the intended change effectively to all stakeholders.
 b. Create an advisory committee.
 c. Find supporters with influence over other stakeholders to help spread the word about the change.
 d. Administer an anonymous survey to see how stakeholders feel about the proposed change.

Constructed Response

1. You are starting your first year as principal at Mendoza High School, which has a diverse student population of about 1,500 students. Over the past several years the pass rate on the state mandated English exam has been declining and is now notably lower than the pass rate in other area high schools. Last school year (prior to your beginning at the school) the English department in conjunction with the faculty audited the school's curriculum and adjusted it to align with the state standards. This year, the superintendent has told you that you will have an additional $12,000 in discretionary funds to support the initiative to increase the pass rate of the English exam. In 300-600 words, outline two important issues you should consider when preparing recommendations for the discretionary budget, explain one strategy you can use to determine budget allocations to recommend that will promote improved student performance, and explain why the strategy you have described will likely be effective.

2. You are the principal of a 900-student middle school (6-8). The school recently formulated a school vision, which includes a critical goal of improving the academic and social-emotional preparedness of the school's eighth-graders for the transition to high school. Over the past several years, teachers and administrators in the local high school have become increasingly concerned about the level of preparedness of entering ninth-grade students. The ninth grades have been increasingly socially immature and lacking in vital academic and study skills. Various stakeholders (parents, students, teachers in both schools) attribute the problem to different reasons and would prescribe different remedies. You form a committee to formulate a plan to improve the readiness of the eighth graders in your school for their transition to high school. Committee members include teachers, parents, student supports (social worker, school psychologist), a special education representative, and a curriculum coordinator.

Write a 150-300 word memo to the members of the committee about the plan to improve eighth grade readiness for high school. Before you write the memo, state what assumptions you make about the school/community (rural/urban, demographics, socioeconomics). In the memo convey why you believe it is important for the school to succeed in this endeavor (improving preparedness for high school), describe 2-3 significant aspects of the school's instructional program that the committee will address in developing its plan. For each of these specific aspects/factors describe a type of data or other information that the team should analyze and explain why this type of information may be useful in analyzing the specific area of concern.

Answer Key and Explanations

Selected Response

1. D: All curriculum and resources should be aligned to standards. Therefore, if standards change, it is likely that the curriculum will need to be revised and new resources purchased. However, before changes in the curriculum can be made, the principal will need to know how the new standards differ from the previous standard. This will help the principal determine if minor revisions to the curriculum are needed or if a new curriculum will need to be adopted.

2. B: School leaders who form data inquiry teams of teachers should direct these teams to develop action plans based on their analyses of student assessment data. They should assign the teams to implement these plans; supporting their implementation (b) is the school leader's job. School leaders should direct teams to analyze data from both formative and summative assessments (c) by classes, student subgroups, and individual students (d).

3. C: This scenario best represents a mutually beneficial relationship. The church has the benefit of having a meeting place and the principal has the benefit of communicating directly with community members on a regular basis. The other activities help to build positive relationships between the school and the community, but are one-sided.

4. A: A school must Manifestation Determination Review within 10 school days according to the following criteria: if the school is seeking to change student placement for more than 10 consecutive days for disciplinary reasons; if the school suspends a student for disciplinary reasons for more than 10 *cumulative,* not consecutive days, *and* for every subsequent suspension, not on a one-time basis; the school is *considering* expelling or otherwise excluding a student for disciplinary reasons rather than already having done so; or the *parent(s)*, not the school, request(s) this meeting after a disciplinary incident.

5. D: Effective new teacher induction programs should focus on supporting not only the new teachers, but also the school leaders who guide them. This requires offering professional development not only to new teachers, but equally to their mentors, school leaders, and other site leaders. Effective induction programs use research-based and standards-based assessment instruments to assess and inform new teacher performance. The ultimate goal of teacher induction programs that make teachers more effective is to improve student achievement.

6. D: School system guidelines recommend that, in giving teachers observational feedback, school leaders should focus feedback discussions by developing open-ended questions that target specific areas for each teacher, explicitly name two or three teacher strengths they observed, identify one area for improvement that will make the most impact on student learning and teacher development, and develop a few specific and attainable next steps for each teacher to take. Effective observational feedback should include strengths and weaknesses and recommendations for next steps should be clear and attainable.

7. D: Because research studies repeatedly prove student benefits of smaller class sizes, school leaders must hire and retain adequate *human* resources in terms of quantity and quality. For a safe, comfortable teaching and learning environment, school leaders must provide adequate *physical* resources like space, furniture, lighting, temperature control, etc. They must manage *fiscal* resources well to manage *all* other resources, not just some.

15

8. C: Curriculum and instruction must be aligned to assessment because what is taught must be measured and what is measured must be taught. If instruction is not aligned to the assessment, it is likely that there will be no measurement of how well students mastered what was taught. Additionally, if instruction is not aligned to the assessment, it is likely that students will be assessed on concepts and material that they have not been taught. Neither of the scenarios is fair or beneficial to students.

9. D: Hiring a coach that can train teachers to use differentiated instruction and evaluate them for efficacy would be the most effective strategy for increasing the uses of differentiated instruction on campus. An instructional coach can provide individual and collective support and can monitor and encourage continuous implementation of the strategy. Praising teachers who implement differentiated instruction creates a positive climate but does not help teachers who do not know how to implement differentiated instruction to do so. Similarly, providing resources and modeling are not sufficient actions to take to increase the use of differentiated instruction if teachers do not know how to implement it or do not see the benefit in implementing the strategy.

10. B: Effective induction programs offered by the New Teacher Center and others have impacts on schools of making new teachers more effective, increasing teacher retention rates, strengthening teacher leadership, addressing education inequities, *and* increasing student learning and achievement.

11. A: Student performance data is a valuable source of data for determining teacher efficacy. Effective instruction should result in student academic growth and satisfactory performance. Survey data and self- assessments can inform support and professional development for teachers but are not as useful in teacher evaluations due to their qualitative and subjective nature.

12. A: To realize instructional change over time, professional development (PD) must be provided on an ongoing basis and reinforced through repetition and classroom follow-up activities. Teachers need theoretical understanding not only of the theory underling instructional practices, but also of how they can apply theory to practice. PD is best administered as a component of a comprehensive, systematic, district-supported educational reform process. When school leaders furnish PD, they should be careful to avoid topics lacking research support, unrelated to student learning, and popular new fads.

13. D: Reducing the teachers' teaching styles is not a priority as long as the teacher is effective at achieving standards in the curriculum. Reducing variability in classrooms throughout the school tends to promote efficiency in purchasing, and in producing testing materials, since each department can use the same materials. This also could allow for benchmarking from class to class, which helps with pacing the curriculum throughout the year. Other procedures and policies, such as bathroom policies or electronic device policies can promote safety by making sure each student is accounted for.

14. D: Effective curricular programs will help students grow academically. Meeting academic performance standards may not be a good indicator of appropriate curricular programs if there is a population of students on campus who are consistently exceeding the performance standards on assessments. Meeting only minimum standards would be a cause of concern and these students would need a curricular program that extends their learning and supports their academic growth. In contrast, an effective curricular program would foster academic growth for all students.

15. D: While school leaders promote a college-bound culture, they also know that students should be prepared for the career of their choice, which may require specialized training or preparation

16

other than traditional college. In this scenario, the school leader should analyze employment data for the community that the school serves and determine if trends in the data justify adding or changing school programming to meet the needs of the community.

16. A: Data must be compared from one point in time to another to determine progress. Benchmark tests are typically used to assess objectives taught during a certain period and do not necessarily assess the same objectives from test to test; therefore, benchmark scores would not necessarily compare the same data to determine progress. Student portfolios from multiple marking periods would provide an assessment of authentic student performance over time and would be most helpful in determining student progress.

17. A: Researchers have found that students' academic self-concepts are *not correlated* with their academic achievement, but *are* correlated with later life successes like employment and earnings. Although socioeconomic status (SES) is related to academic self-concept (as well as achievement and retention), it does *not* correlate as strongly with SES as with students' home educational settings. Although smaller school size is found to benefit student participation as well as principal leadership and teacher distributed leadership, *larger* school size correlates positively with student academic self-concept.

18. C: Group consensus is an ideal approach for collaborative decisions in that all participants' voices are heard, and every member must provide input and agree with the group decision. However, it is more time-consuming, not more time-efficient, than majority rule or committee decision-making. Majority rule is the method wherein minority voters' commitment can be undermined. Committee decision-making is the method whereby committee members may feel their time and effort were wasted if members of the larger group frequently override committee decisions.

19. D: Structured observations, which may be conducted by peers, leaders, or others, are collaborative as they involve the teachers being observed, those observing them, and the feedback and other interaction they share based on and following observations. Conducting action research, reflection during teaching practice, and reading current research in their field are professional development activities that teachers can engage in individually.

20. C: The PLC will include teachers in the same grade level in different subjects which is horizontal alignment. The PLC will also include teachers in different grade levels in the same subject which is vertical alignment. Consequently, this PLC is an example of both horizontal and vertical alignment of curriculum and instruction.

21. B: The principal should determine which professional development sessions that teachers are attending and whether those sessions are aligned to the curriculum, instruction, and programs on campus. The professional development sessions may be informative but may not be practically applicable to the campus if they are not aligned with campus goals. For example, if a teacher attends a professional development session on project-based learning, yet the campus does not implement nor support project-based learning, there will be little to no evidence of changes in instructional practice on campus as a result of attendance to that session.

22. A: The number of math and reading teachers and the size of their classes most directly impact student learning. Research has demonstrated that class size is an influencing factor of student performance and that reducing class sizes to assist struggling students has also shown to be effective. School start time, testing intervals, and access to technology indirectly impact student learning.

23. B: Recognizing and celebrating educational success is an effective strategy to develop positive family and community partnerships. A school leader should make an effort to organize events on campus and in the community to develop positive partnerships. Live events facilitate two-way communication, unlike newsletters which are one-way modes of communication. Attending athletic events and soliciting feedback from the community are additional ways to build a relationship with the community, but the most effective strategy for building a positive partnership is to host an event that spotlights positive things related to the school and students.

24. A: Formative data helps teachers to assess their effectiveness during instruction (rather than after) and accordingly make adjustments to improve student outcomes. Summative data can assist teachers in identifying areas of improvement in their teaching practice but is often too late to identify specific remedial student groups. Student profiles from permanent records (e.g., demographics, assessment histories, family information, etc.) give less detailed information provide less information to inform instruction. Enrollment data helps educators identify budgetary needs and student demographic distributions, but do not inform instruction, staff development, remedial student groups, or information plans.

25. D: School leaders should not analyze only ethical implications of decisions for the school community (a) but habituate every member to such analysis to guide their approaches. Because total experience and learning contribute to their development, ethical frameworks should grow throughout school leaders' careers, not remain constant (b). Ethical school leaders never accept funding from donors requiring less effective methods (c). By regularly engaging staff and stakeholders in conversations helping them self-examine assumptions and develop ethical understanding (d), school leaders integrate ethical discussion into school culture.

26. B: The dean should ask teachers what resources they would like and purchase as many of their suggestions as possible for all teachers. This would increase the number of resources available to teachers and offer them a variety of resources to choose from. Requiring teachers to purchase materials on their own is a disincentive if teachers cannot afford the upfront cost. Professional development is not a resource, it is training. Seeking free or discounted materials does not guarantee that the number and variety of resources will increase on campus if there are limited to no resources available in the local area.

27. D: School funding comes from a variety of sources. The federal government provides some funding, but this funding is usually unsubstantial and may fluctuate due to the changing budget decisions at the federal level. The state governments also provide funding to schools based on income and/or sales taxes. The majority of school funding is gained from property taxes within the school district. Both residences and commercial properties are taxed, and a portion of those taxes are allocated to school districts. Schools and school districts often seek grants and donations from foundations to supplement the school's budget.

28. B: Novice teachers need increased support. Facilitating collaboration between teachers and encouraging team teaching provides support for teachers while simultaneously improving the quality of instruction delivered to students. Monitoring data, conducting observations, offering feedback, and providing tutorials to students are beneficial actions, but are reactive to deficits in instruction. The principal is being proactive by facilitating collaborative teaching so that students will receive good instruction in the classroom.

29. A: Differentiated instruction refers to providing customized or tailored instruction to students to meet their diverse learning needs. Previous academic performance, special needs (such as a physical or learning disability), and learning styles are good ways to determine how to differentiate

18

instruction to meet student needs. Other sources of data, such as interests, career goals, and others can be helpful, but are not always relevant.

30. C: Depending on school budget and resources, student needs that are not directly related to student safety and academic performance may not be able to be addressed using school resources. Many community resources used to support schools are targeted toward students in need. These types of resources may address physical needs of students and their families, such as providing food, clothing, toiletries, haircuts and grooming, or helping adults find jobs.

31. D: The least restrictive environment for a student who receives special education services is the same environment as their peers who do not receive these services. Any time a student is removed from the main program of education, their environment is restricted. A students LRE is determined by their Individualized Education Plan and may differ based on their learning needs. However, a student's IEP and academic performance must be reviewed regularly to ensure that the student is in the least restrictive environment possible.

32. B: Testing accommodations for some students based on their individual needs are not unfair, but actually make assessments fairer and also more valid. School leaders can help decrease achievement gaps among student cultural groups and backgrounds by using student data to monitor progress regularly. However, extensive testing of students, especially to the impediment of instruction, can be detrimental to students who are already low performing. Data collected from assessments, even non-standardized formative assessments, can be used to monitor student progress and inform instructional decisions.

33. A: Expert recommendations for school leaders in the best use of school-wide student achievement data include instituting supports for developing a data-driven school culture (a); instructing students to understand and use their own data (b) to set learning goals; developing and maintaining data systems on a district-wide basis (c); and incorporating data as an essential component of a cycle of continuous instructional improvement (d).

34. A: The Supportive School Discipline Initiative (SSDI) included guidance for positive school discipline practices to keep students in school by providing alternatives to exclusionary methods like suspension and expulsion. This guidance was produced jointly by the US Departments of Education and Justice to ensure enforcement of federal civil rights protections against discrimination. It provides school resources with helpful information rather than getting it from them. The SSDI's purpose was to keep student discipline from escalating to the police or prison systems, not to continue this trend.

35. A: A school leader must create structures in the school programming that promote collaboration for teachers. Allotting time in the master schedule for co-planning ensures that teachers will have dedicated time to collaborate, such as by participating in professional learning communities. Offering to pay teachers to stay after school may not be effective because some teachers may opt-out. Additionally, these planning sessions could interfere with other school activities these teachers may be involved in, such as coaching or tutoring. Providing asynchronous collaboration online could potentially be helpful, but it is not the best choice since it likely will not lead to real-time collaboration. Removing qualified teachers for planning can negatively impact student performance and should be used sparingly, if at all.

36. B: The Civil Rights Act of 1964 (a) protects everyone, including students, against discrimination for multiple reasons. The Americans with Disabilities Act (ADA, 1973) protects individuals against discrimination for disabilities; Title II of the ADA Amendments Act of 2008 (c) protects students

19

with disabilities from discrimination by requiring equal opportunities to benefit from government programs, services, and activities, including education. Section 504 of the Rehabilitation Act of 1973, amended 2003 (d), also protects students with disabilities against discrimination. The 1974 Family Educational Rights and Privacy Act (FERPA) protects student education records privacy; the Individuals with Disabilities Act (IDEA) does this for students with disabilities (b).

37. D: Focused discussions and effective interaction between students are indicators that the instructional activities are effective. Student discourse, whether teacher-facilitated or independent, is an indicator or learning and mastery of content. Increased student attendance is a positive student outcome but is not necessarily the direct result of a particular instructional activity. Differentiated instruction and flexible student grouping are instructional strategies, not outcomes.

38. D: A coach is a professional who helps a teacher develop the skills necessary to do their job effectively. A coach is a staff member who does not supervise or evaluate the person being coached. This helps to foster a relationship of trust between the coach and the teacher. A coach will identify a teacher's areas of strength and weakness based on a predetermined rubric or set of expectations. Then the coach will provide one-on-one support to the teacher to help improve targeted areas. A coach may provide books and resources, recommend professional development sessions, model effective teaching methods, observe the teacher in practice to provide real-time feedback, assist in the lesson planning process, and guide the teacher in self-reflection and critical analysis processes. A coach provides individualized, targeted support to teachers and helps them to grow, usually in a shorter period of time than other forms of professional development support.

39. C: All levels, from individual schools to state education departments, must ultimately align with federal policy to make major educational goals match the national vision. However, within this hierarchy, specific expressions of policy, e.g., standardized test instruments, reflect the next higher level. Thus, state standardized tests reflect federal standards, not just state standards; individual schools *directly* apply standards from their school systems, not state standards, which in turn reflect the standards of their school districts, which in turn *directly* apply state standards, not federal standards.

40. A: Classroom observations, student class grades, and summative assessment data would be the best sources of data to provide feedback to teachers to improve student learning. Data sources for improving teaching and learning should include instructional delivery (classroom observations) and student performance outcomes. Both formative and summative assessment data can be used to determine student mastery of objectives and efficacy of instructional delivery.

41. D: New policies should be well communicated in vision and in methodology, but if the policy comes directly from the leadership without having shared motivation the community as a whole will not have buy in and the implementation is likely to face resistance. Delegating authority to staff is a great way of involving stakeholders within the school building but does not include members of the school community who are not employed at the school. Communicating frequently is effective for sharing the vision but does not necessarily motivate community members to participate in implementing new ideas, policies, and procedures.

42. A: To gather this kind of feedback, the school leader should develop specific questions that are critical in nature and appropriate to this topic. Open-ended questions will stimulate discussions of many other stakeholder issues and concerns (b). Interviewing them all (c) is impracticable or at best very time inefficient. Discussion meetings (d) are both less focused like (b) and less time effective, like (c).

43. B: Researchers found that, among public schools, those with higher performance than others each seemed to have a unique combination of factors contributing to their success. These factors include having a clear and shared focus, having high expectations and standards for students, and high levels of family and community involvement. An effective school leader is a significant factor in high performing schools but is not the only determinant of success. Similarly, alignment of curriculum and instruction and frequent monitoring of teaching and learning are critical success factors but cannot be deemed the most important. Finally, school need resources for success, but many public schools have demonstrated success with meager funding.

44. B: Reading and writing skills are best taught and reinforced within the context of subject matter content. Creating a cross-curricular focus on reading and writing skills would best address the gap in performance among students who are not reading on grade level. Increasing opportunities for students to read is beneficial, but is less effective in closing opportunity gaps, especially when opportunities to engage in reading are voluntary such as after school or at home. Targeted test preparation has limited efficacy if attendance is voluntary and student performance is not monitored.

45. D: School principals should remain objective when observing teachers, regardless of their tenure or contract status. An evaluation rubric for teacher assessment should be used fairly and objectively for all teachers. A principal should observe what assignments the teacher gives the students, whether they are actively implementing new strategies, and the overall classroom environment and culture.

46. B: Community resources can be used in a variety of ways, such as providing school supplies for students, facilitating field trips, and providing mentorship. However, providing tutorial services to students most directly supports student learning. Tutoring students directly impacts student academic performance in class, whereas the other community resources support students' economic and psychosocial needs that may only impact learning indirectly.

47. C: A successful new teacher induction program will provide opportunities for new teachers to collaborate with one another and with more experienced teachers. Additionally, a successful program will incorporate leadership development opportunities for new teachers to explore and refine their leadership skills. New teachers should receive strategic professional coaching and be assigned a mentor based on experience and effectiveness of the mentoring staff member. While the school leader is responsible for ensuring that an effective induction program in place, there are other instructional staff and campus leaders who can add value to the induction program by facilitating various aspects of the program.

48. B: In most public-school districts, typically the District Office of Achievement and Accountability makes preliminary enrollment projections to inform school budgets, but not alone because of the difficulty of projecting. Instead, they submit their projections to school leaders, who revise them as needed. School leaders do not project their schools' enrollment alone. Final enrollment projections are made by district committees representing not only the Finance and Student Support offices, but also district Achievement and Accountability and Operations offices.

49. A: Leaders should use as many opportunities as possible to observe staff performance in order to have a well-rounded view of their performance. The opportunities may include various days of the week, times of the day, and varied circumstances. A leader should be intentional and deliberate about seeking different opportunities to observe staff at a variety of times in a variety of circumstances in order to obtain a fair and holistic view of staff performance.

50. D: All of these factors are important to consider, but the leader must first ensure that the professional development will help staff meet the vision and goals that have already been established. A leader needs to be deliberate in selecting professional development for staff members so that the professional development is purposeful in helping staff achieve the campus goals and vision.

51. C: The best action that the principal can take to increase the frequency of classroom observations is to plan the observations into the schedule each week. This will force all other appointments and meetings to be scheduled around the classroom observations. Classroom visits should not be left to chance or they will likely not be conducted due to the many tasks that a principal may have to address throughout the day. Additionally, the principal should aim to visit classrooms on different days of the week and times of the day to obtain a well-rounded perspective of teaching and learning on campus.

52. A: All students receiving perfect scores for 18 consecutive weeks may be an indication that the students are not receiving rigorous curriculum and instruction. While there is an expectation for students to be successful in the classroom, there is low statistical likelihood that all students would perform perfectly over extended periods of time if they were receiving instruction at or above their level. Each student should receive a rigorous curriculum which means delivering instruction at an appropriate level of challenge in order to grow students academically.

53. D: The American Psychological Association (APA) recommends a tiered model of behavior management above all others for schools—i.e., a system of positive behavior supports that includes both prevention and intervention with primary, secondary, and tertiary levels—not only for school-wide systems or only for disruptive behaviors of individual students, but for both of these as well as for classroom behavior management.

54. A: The Individuals with Disabilities Education Act (IDEA) and Family Rights and Privacy Act (FERPA) both define the same document types as educational records (b). FERPA determines conditions for educational records destruction based on state laws (c). IDEA amendments regarding educational records collection, maintenance, confidentiality, disclosure (d), and destruction (c) are based on FERPA. However, the IDEA requires designating special education records custodians to ensure the instruction and training of all educators collecting confidential information, but FERPA does not (a).

55. B: The action that would best address the challenges in communication, parental engagement, and at home learning is to help the parents learn English by offering ESL classes on campus. Hosting the classes on campus encourages parents to engage with the school community and reinforces that the school values the presence and engagement of the parents. Having a translator on campus and translating documents for parents are important actions to take but are not long-term solutions to the challenge. Students should not be asked to translate school information for their parents.

56. A: Requesting that teachers identify student work and post it, then reviewing the posted work demonstrates that the school leader wants to be involved in analyzing student work. The posted work will provide the school leader with an assessment of student performance as well as what teachers consider to be exemplary work. This request does not directly encourage teacher collaboration as teachers could make autonomous decisions regarding their students' performance. Additionally, the request does not directly exemplify an assessment of alignment to standards. Finally, not all students are recognized, only students who performed in an exemplary manner.

57. D: Experts recommend that school leaders not simply complete a checklist for classroom visits (a) but further student success through improving teacher instructional quality by applying their observations of classroom instructional practices. School leaders should give both individual teachers feedback, through conversations and written communications, and collective teacher feedback (b), through providing statistics (d). They can produce formative feedback through making walk-throughs (c) and both formative and summative feedback through making formal observations.

58. B: School leaders can promote equitable access to curriculum for all students and parents by making staff more comfortable discussing diversity issues, social justice, and values, which will promote equity; clarifying staff misconceptions related to deficit theories about minorities and diverse groups; modeling equity beliefs and behaviors in daily interactions; confronting discrimination and stereotyping in actions and language; creating safe school environments where all students feel welcomed and valued; and establishing support networks for students harassed over cultural, sexual, and/or gender identity.

59. A: Rigor in academic instruction refers to curriculum and instruction that is challenging to students. Rigorous instruction challenges students academically, but also intellectually and even personally. Rigorous instruction is often complex and challenges students to think deeply and critically. Rigor does not mean excessively hard or difficult. However, rigor does involve instruction that is stimulating and engaging. Rigorous instruction often requires students to make connections across academic content areas and apply concepts to the real world.

60. C: School principals should look for evidence of learning when conducting a classroom observation. Students should be given opportunities to respond and demonstrate learning throughout the lesson so that the teacher and the observer can determine whether students are learning the content. These opportunities may occur as questioning strategies, discussion, or through guided and independent practice. It is important for teachers to be comfortable with the instructional content and method of delivery, but this is not a primary focus of a classroom observation as a novice teacher can be nervous yet still effective. Additionally, the physical classroom setup should be conducive to learning but is not the primary focus of a classroom observation.

61. A: A supportive school climate occurs when students have resources readily available to them that can help them feel supported and to overcome challenges that they may face. The resources available should be based on student needs, such as counseling, mentorship, social activities, and others. A supportive school climate should foster peer relationships among peers intentionally rather than allowing them to happen by chance because students share common schedules. While policy handbooks for students are useful, they do not directly contribute to a supportive school environment. On the other hand, student interactions with adults on campus can directly impact students' feelings of being supported.

62. B: Researchers have found that the most effective school leaders have powerful influences over student achievement and school effectiveness; that these influences are indirect (a); that today's schools cannot be led by one principal without other educators' participating significantly (b); that the traditional model of single formal leadership neglects utilizing the valuable expertise of teachers (c); and that it is harder to sustain programs and improvements instituted under one principal after that principal leaves the school (d).

63. A: The primary benefit of evaluating staff members is to provide an opportunity for leaders to identify areas of strength and weakness among the staff and to provide constructive feedback to staff members so that they can grow professionally. Leaders can use these evaluations to determine what additional support and resources need to be provided to support or improve the performance of staff members.

64. C: Professional learning communities allow staff with shared roles or responsibilities to collaborate in a way that meets the needs of teachers and students. These communities are usually goal-driven and encourage the sharing of ideas and responsibilities. Professional learning communities are used in a variety of ways, but the primary purpose is to facilitate collaboration among educators.

65. C: Evaluating and revising campus-based assessments to ensure alignment to standards demonstrates a commitment to school-wide rigorous instruction. Assessments should accurately measure the standards. Increasing the offering of advanced placement and dual credit courses supports rigorous curriculum for some students who qualify, but does not impact rigor school wide. Similarly, increasing participation in college entrance exams does not raise the rigor of instruction on campus, but encourages students to seek and prepare for college admittance.

66. C: The school board hires and supervises the superintendent, who in turns hires and supervises the school principal. In the hierarchy of public education leadership, the school board makes policy decisions based on state and local legislature and the superintendent implements these policies. School principals apply these policies to the daily operations of the school. There may be instances in which a principal participates in a school board meeting, such as by reporting data or speaking, but these activities are not part of the regular responsibilities of a principal in relation to the school board.

67. A: Fundraisers are a common way for schools to secure money and resources outside of school budgets. Fundraisers should always be conducted within the policies and procedures outlined by the school campus and the school district.

68. D: One of the foundations of a professional learning community is identifying the standards and curriculum that must be taught and ensuring that the curriculum is delivered effectively. A question that PLC members must ask is "What do we want students to learn?". Answering this question ensures that the standards-based curriculum is prioritized, and that formative and summative assessment is a reflection of the curriculum that is taught.

69. C: Effective school leaders involve all students in developing systems for collecting, analyzing, applying, incorporating, and sharing data rather than only identifying some students to involve (a); involve all staff members in participating in developing assessment plans rather than designating certain members (b); involve students closely in knowing and monitoring their own data (c); and basing individual student goals on each student's specific data measures, not just on overall school data (d).

70. A: Leaders intent on fostering change or being agents of change are required to strategically communicate the intended change and gather supporters for that change. First, the leader needs to communicate the intended change effectively. Many people are unwilling to support changes because they fear the unknown. The leader should communicate not only what is to be changed but also how the changes affect the various staff members and how the changes are aligned to the school vision and goals.

Practice Test #2

Selected Response

1. Which of the following would provide the most valid indication of a culture of high expectations?

- a. Setting campus goals above minimum standards
- b. Hosting award ceremonies for high- achieving students
- c. Recognizing the Teacher of the Year publicly
- d. Holding regular community meetings to discuss school performance with stakeholders

2. Which of the following is the most critical question to consider when using community resources in the classroom?

- a. Are the resources aligned with the curriculum?
- b. Are there enough resources for all students?
- c. Are teachers familiar with these resources?
- d. Are the resources expected to be returned?

3. Which of the following is the best example of a school leader providing a safe environment for teacher to express their beliefs and ideas?

- a. Scheduling monthly one-on-one meetings with individual teachers.
- b. Placing a suggestion box in the teachers' lounge.
- c. Administering an electronic survey to campus staff to obtain feedback.
- d. Providing collaborative meeting time for teachers and meeting with them regularly to discuss their ideas.

4. To assist teachers with integrating technology into instruction, which should school leaders do?

- a. Lead teachers first to encourage student technology use for enhancing research skills
- b. Lead teachers to avoid legal and ethical issues with technology as outside their scope
- c. Lead teachers to encourage student concept comprehension before using technology
- d. Lead teachers to target technology skills and content quality without differentiation

5. Which of the following is most accurate about effective and appropriate school and co-curricular activities to prepare high school students for college and careers?

- a. Career and technical education can only be obtained in magnet or technical schools.
- b. School partnerships with higher education institutions best prepare students for jobs.
- c. Community-based and project-based learning prepare students for higher education.
- d. High school curricula should be pertinent to student lives, communities, and cultures.

6. An assistant principal analyzes student performance data for the grading period and notices that a class of students consistently performs well in Reading and has not demonstrated growth. What might this data suggest?

- a. The data is evidence of academic dishonesty.
- b. The students may need more rigorous instruction.
- c. The teacher is ineffective.
- d. Classroom instruction and assessment are unaligned.

25

7. In many public-school districts, students with certain linguistic and/or cultural backgrounds are disproportionately enrolled in special education programs. How can a school leader best address this type of overrepresentation?

a. Examine current school procedures for assigning grade levels to students
b. Examine instructional strategies targeting students referred to special education
c. Examine instruments used to evaluate student need for special education
d. Examine the curriculum and related expectations of student achievement

8. Which of the following best illustrates the connection between the school community and local employment trends?

a. A school begins to offer health care courses and training in response to a need for more healthcare workers in the community.
b. The school librarian partners with the neighborhood library to share resources.
c. A school sets a goal to increase the graduation rate.
d. A school increases the number of dual-credit college courses offered on campus.

9. Which of the following practices by school leaders most effectively improves teacher practice and student learning?

a. Reviewing student performance data and sharing aggregated results with teachers.
b. Administering self-assessment surveys to teachers.
c. Conducting regular classroom observations and providing timely feedback.
d. Offering educational resources to teachers related to their identified areas of weakness.

10. Which of these is a valid guideline for school leaders to support staff throughout their professional development (PD)?

a. To be job-embedded and school-based, PD must occur in the school building.
b. For effective PD, teachers must not learn passively, but be actively involved.
c. Because teachers are the ones involved in PD, it should be teacher-centered.
d. PD must be done independently to ensure individual learning and growth.

11. Which of the following best represents transparent decision-making?

a. The principal meets with a focus group prior to making a decision.
b. The principal administers a survey and considers the data prior to making a decision.
c. The principal informs the community that a decision needs to be made about eliminating the dance program and shares data that may impact the decision.
d. The principal posts meeting minutes from committee meetings online.

12. A school leader is developing a plan for improving teaching on campus and has identified several effective teachers in the math department. How should the school leader best incorporate these teachers into the plan?

a. Request that the teachers mentor low-performing teachers.
b. Allow the teachers to continue teaching using their current best practices.
c. Recognize the teachers for their effective performance.
d. Allow the teachers to identify areas in which they would like to grow and provide resources and support.

13. The school principal had a meeting unexpectedly be cancelled and decided to use the free time to engage in activities on campus related to curriculum and instruction. Which of the following activities should the principal choose to engage in?

    a. Assist with lunch duty.
    b. Identify students to tutor in a small group.
    c. Visit professional learning committees to engage in discussion regarding student progress.
    d. Analyze student performance data from the most recent benchmark assessment.

14. Which of the following accurately reflects evaluative criteria that school leaders should consider first when deciding to utilize community resources to support student learning?

    a. Congruence with the school's vision and mission.
    b. Immediate impact on student achievement.
    c. Results from prior implementation.
    d. The relationship of the person or organization to the school.

15. A newly appointed principal has been advised that the teachers on campus are disgruntled and resistant to change. Which of the following is the best action for the principal to take first to address this issue?

    a. Send out a survey to all teachers to assess campus culture.
    b. Meet with a focus group of teacher leaders and allow them to voice their concerns.
    c. Hold an all-staff meeting and communicate the vision for the school.
    d. Send an email to all teachers informing them of new policies and procedures.

16. Which of the following have education researchers identified as important regarding implementation of school-wide data initiatives??

    a. More training opportunities and promotion of the data system in implementation are most effective.
    b. Technology that supports data initiatives offers the answer to data use in schools.
    c. Individual teachers utilize data technology systems more quickly and productively.
    d. The success of a school data initiative is determined by the data system selected.

17. A high school principal ensured that the campus was fully staffed with highly qualified teachers at least a month before the start of the school year. What is the primary benefit of this effort?

    a. Teachers who are hired early have more time to prepare for the school year.
    b. Personnel budgets must be submitted before the school year begins.
    c. All teachers will have an opportunity to participate in trainings and professional development prior to the start of the year.
    d. Teachers who are hired later in the year have classroom management issues.

18. Which of the following is most used in self-assessment to facilitate professional development?

    a. Teachers write in journals about their work.
    b. Teachers apply advice they receive to work.
    c. Teachers analyze videos of their instruction.
    d. Teachers benefit from others' experiences.

19. A high school principal has created instructional teams comprised of teachers from each core content area and fine arts. These teams plan instruction together and incorporate concepts from the various subjects in each of their classrooms. This strategy is an example of what type of instruction?

    a. Differentiated instruction
    b. Rigorous instruction
    c. Cross-curricular instruction
    d. Professional learning communities

20. Which of the following is true about school leaders as role models for teachers in professional development (PD)?

    a. School leaders should facilitate PD activities.
    b. School leaders should participate in PD with teachers.
    c. School leaders should monitor teacher implementation of learning from PD sessions.
    d. School leaders should determine the PD offered to teachers.

21. The Dean of Instruction analyzed data from the most recent benchmark assessment and noticed that when the data was disaggregated by race and ethnicity, a particular group failed to meet performance standards. How should the dean address this?

    a. Talk to teachers who instruct the demographic group and students that belong to the demographic group to identify the challenges they are facing in mastering the content.
    b. Contact the parents of the students who were not successful and inform them that their child needs tutoring.
    c. Observe the teachers who instruct the demographic group to determine their efficacy.
    d. Develop a schedule of tutorials and remediation for the students who did not master the content.

22. Which of the following best describes how school leaders of more effective schools assign students to new (i.e., novice or beginning) teachers, compared to their more experienced colleagues?

    a. In more effective schools, new teachers are assigned students with lower achievement.
    b. In more effective schools, new teachers are assigned students with higher achievement.
    c. In more effective schools, new teachers are assigned randomly relative to achievement.
    d. In more effective schools, new teachers are assigned students with similar achievement.

23. Which of the following is correct about effective classroom management systems?

    a. Tiered positive behavior support models provide both prevention and intervention.
    b. Tiered positive behavior support models are only for preventing behavior problems.
    c. Tiered positive behavior support models are designed to be behavior interventions.
    d. Tiered positive behavior support models provide less time in academic engagement.

24. As part of an overall school reform initiative, a principal makes a plan to distribute leadership among educators and other stakeholders for implementing school goals. Which research findings exist to inform this decision?

    a. Distributing leadership improves professional development but nothing else.
    b. Educational reform changes demand efforts requiring a few superior leaders.
    c. The capacity building needed for school improvement limits leader numbers.
    d. School reform initiatives all share implicit distributed leadership in common.

25. Which of the following is true regarding information and data that teachers should consider when planning for differentiated instruction?

    a. Special population identification and past academic performance are the only data that teachers should consider when planning for differentiated instruction.

    b. Formative assessment is not useful when planning for differentiated instruction.

    c. Student interests should be a major determining factor when planning for differentiated instruction.

    d. Student performance data, interests, and learning styles should all be considered when planning for differentiated instruction.

26. Which of the following professional development activities would likely have the most impact on current teacher performance?

    a. A self-paced book study program for all teachers.

    b. Online courses that teachers select and participate in individually at their own pace.

    c. A four-hour in-person training conducted during the school year.

    d. A hybrid online and in-person six-week course that meets weekly for a cohort of teachers.

27. To evaluate teacher effectiveness in applying instructional strategies, school leaders need a working knowledge of student-centered, research-based teaching methods. What is most true about these?

    a. The Socratic method is a useful, research-based strategy for delivering instruction.

    b. Project-based learning requires technology integration in order to be implemented effectively.

    c. Cooperative learning has been proven to be an effective, research-based instructional strategy.

    d. It is necessary for teachers to utilize technology to deliver instruction in order to be effective.

28. A school leader is developing a process for continuous improvement on campus. Which of the following actions should the school leader take first?

    a. Develop evaluation procedures and set checkpoints for evaluation.

    b. Train staff on the continuous improvement process.

    c. Select a low performing area that needs to be addressed.

    d. Identify strategies for addressing low performing areas.

29. Which of the following factors may directly affect a school leader's ability to recruit and retain highly qualified teachers?

    a. The number of recruitment fairs that a school leader attends

    b. The percentage of experienced teachers already on campus

    c. The school culture

    d. The available technology on campus

30. The leadership team of an elementary school has implemented a new math software program for all students in grades three through five. After three months of using the program, the students participated in a district benchmark exam and they showed little to no growth in math performance overall. What step should the leadership team take next?

  a. Abandon the program because it is not effective.
  b. Develop a plan for monitoring the math program at shorter intervals to determine its efficacy.
  c. Reduce the number of students using the math program.
  d. Increase the amount of time that students use the program.

31. The principal has noted that Mr. Smith, a star teacher, arrives late to school every day. The assistant principal who supervises Mr. Smith informs the principal that no one bothers Mr. Smith about his late arrival because he does such a great job in the classroom. The assistant principal's action is a violation of:

  a. fairness.
  b. integrity.
  c. justice.
  d. trust.

32. What does research into school mental health show about collaboration with the community?

  a. Clinical psychiatric care and other services are not practicable or suitable in schools.
  b. A cohesive continuum of intervention must primarily address severe mental health problems.
  c. School staff must work with families and service providers rather than policymakers.
  d. An integrated intervention continuum must mainly address universal student need.

33. The Dean of Instruction conducted a classroom observation of a 7th grade math teacher and noticed that the math teacher was not following the curriculum for the math department. When asked, the math teacher informed the dean that the students were not ready for the standards identified in the curriculum and that he chose to review standards from 6th grade instead.

Which of the following would be the best response from the dean to the math teacher?

  a. Commend the math teacher for addressing the gaps in student learning.
  b. Require that the math teacher attend training on the math curriculum.
  c. Model instruction of the standards outlined in the curriculum.
  d. Direct the math teacher to teach the standards outlined in the curriculum.

34. Which of the following best describes what school leaders should consider when identifying professional development for staff?

  a. Individual staff members' goals are most important.
  b. School goals and vision always take precedence.
  c. Individual staff member and school goals are of equal importance.
  d. Professional development is primarily for accountability purposes and goals.

35. According to multiple research studies, what is a characteristic of school leaders related to evaluating teacher effectiveness?

a. The most effective school leaders are better at identifying the best candidates for hiring as teachers.
b. The most effective school leaders are better at identifying the best and worst teachers on their staff.
c. The most effective teachers are attracted to the schools whose leaders have hired the best teachers.
d. The most effective school leaders are better at identifying better and average teachers than poorer ones.

36. What trends in student achievement data would be the best indicator that there are problems in curriculum alignment?

a. Students perform well on campus-based tests but perform poorly on college entrance exams.
b. Students earn satisfactory grades on school report cards but perform poorly on standardized tests.
c. Students with disabilities perform poorly on campus-based tests.
d. Students who have a history of high academic performance show little to no growth on standardized tests.

37. In public school districts, which personnel are *not* likely to be directly supervised by the campus principal?

a. Bus drivers.
b. Custodians.
c. Volunteers.
d. Cafeteria workers.

38. Several teachers on campus have expressed concerns to the principal that there is too much focus on standardized assessment. The teachers suggest that they develop authentic assessments for student learning. Which of the following is the best example of authentic summative assessment?

a. Benchmark tests
b. Student choice of completing a project, essay, or performance
c. Oral exams
d. Allowing students to complete homework assignments at their own pace

39. Advanced technology integration in schools includes empowering students to engage in the learning process using technology. Which of the following best exemplifies students creating content using digital media?

a. Students access wiki pages to review lesson materials
b. Students record themselves reading aloud for reading assessment
c. Students design elaborate digital storybooks to prepare for a state writing exam
d. Students create PowerPoint presentations about insects using photos from the internet

40. For a school principal to assess the effectiveness of his or her strategies to communicate the school vision, which method would be MOST informative?

    a. Separately ask a group of students and a group of parents what the vision is; see if answers align.

    b. Separately ask the teachers and a group of parents to state the vision, and compare their answers.

    c. Separately ask different members of the school staff to articulate the vision, comparing responses.

    d. Separately ask an educational leader, student, teacher, and parent the vision; see if answers align.

41. Which of the following accurately describes cognitive and affective processes involved in school organizational learning and staff development?

    a. Conversation and affirmation are cognitive, reflection and invitation are affective.

    b. Reflection and conversation are cognitive, affirmation and invitation are affective.

    c. Reflection and affirmation are cognitive, conversation and invitation are affective.

    d. Affirmation and invitation are cognitive, reflection and conversation are affective.

42. Among school leader responsibilities for managing daily school facility operations, which is MOST likely to involve district support for hiring expert consultants to address contemporary issues?

    a. Managing the food services in the school

    b. Managing school environmental quality

    c. Managing school transportation services

    d. Managing custodial services in a school

43. For the third subsequent year, a school leader has had 40 percent turnover of teaching staff. This high rate of turnover has impacted the campus negatively and the school leader wants to address this concern. In a stakeholder meeting, the leader asks members to brainstorm suggestions for addressing teacher retention. Which of the following suggestions should the school leader implement first?

    a. Administer a survey to teachers to get their feedback on what they like and dislike about working at the campus.

    b. Petition the district to raise teacher salaries.

    c. Offer bonuses to teachers who produce good student performance results on standardized assessments.

    d. Provide mentors to new teachers on campus.

44. Research shows that school leaders' time spent on which of these does *not* predict better student achievement?

    a. Making evaluations.

    b. Class walkthroughs.

    c. Coaching teachers.

    d. Program development.

45. Which of the following strategies is least likely to improve teacher practice?

a. Conducting regular classroom observations and providing written feedback to teachers.
b. Pairing novice teachers with an experienced teacher for peer coaching.
c. Providing teachers with aggregated student performance data each grading cycle.
d. Facilitating professional learning communities for teacher collaboration by grade level and by content area.

46. Which of the following represents a potential conflict of interest?

a. A potential contractor for remodeling the gymnasium is a relative of the school principal.
b. The assistant principal's son attends the school where they work.
c. The principal owns a house in the community that the school serves.
d. The math software that the district adopted was used in a school district where the principal served prior.

47. What is the most accurate definition of a learning objective?

a. What educators hope to accomplish during their instruction
b. What educators are supposed instruct the students
c. What students expect teachers to instruct them
d. What educators expect students to be able to do via instruction

48. According to experts, which of the following is the most important factor in how school leaders evaluate their teachers?

a. Being motivated to evaluate teachers.
b. Making time for regular observations.
c. Making time for longer observations.
d. Making evaluations discrete events.

49. A school leader wants to create a risk-taking environment for teachers where they feel comfortable improving their practices for teaching and learning. Which of the following actions should the school leader take to accomplish this goal?

a. Create a system of peer evaluations.
b. Allow teachers to choose their own professional development opportunities.
c. Create a digital data dashboard so teachers can share achievement data with one another.
d. Place a suggestion box in the teachers' lounge.

50. To inform professional development methods, which of the following is the best format for adult learners, based on the principles of adult learning?

a. Formal
b. Directive
c. Hands-on
d. Theoretical

51. Which of the following activities would not be evidence that all students are being prepared for and have access to a challenging curriculum?

   a. Students who were enrolled in pre-advanced placement courses in middle school are automatically enrolled in advanced placement courses in high school.
   b. The school leader regular monitors student performance data on tests and in classes to determine alignment of campus-based assessment to standardized assessment.
   c. All students are administered college entrance exams on the school campus at no cost to the student.
   d. Students who have a history of meeting satisfactory performance standards on standardized tests are offered enrichment courses to help them reach mastery performance levels.

52. Of the following, which is true about multiple assessments of student learning?

   a. Different assessment types access different skills and learning styles.
   b. Students must be re-tested often or they forget what they learned.
   c. Summative assessments following instruction are typically sufficient.
   d. Summative assessments enable adjusting instruction as it continues.

53. A new school principal administered a survey to school staff to assess the perceived culture of the school. The data from the survey showed that most of the staff felt that all ideas for the school came from the top and were forced down. The school principal wants to shift the culture and encourage staff to be innovative. Which of the following strategies would best help the principal to meet this goal?

   a. Create action committees made up of teachers and staff and give the committees time and resources to generate solutions to campus needs.
   b. Place a suggestion box in the teachers' lounge and encourage teachers to submit their ideas for consideration.
   c. Inform the staff that there are positions on the Shared Decision-Making Committee for teachers and that they would feel more represented if they engaged in the process.
   d. Host a town hall meeting and allow participants to share their ideas publicly.

54. Of the following, which accurately reflects a principle of adult learning that applies to professional development (PD) for teachers?

   a. Adults learn best when participation in PD is required.
   b. Adults learn best when learning materials are selected and provided.
   c. Adults learn best when they are involved in planning the instruction.
   d. Adults learn best when informed about how they will be assessed prior to participation.

55. Which of the following is the best example of summative assessment?

   a. Standardized tests
   b. Homework assignments
   c. Practice assignments completed in class
   d. Projects

56. Which of the following describes a role of parents and other community members as it relates to educator professional development (PD)?

    a. Holding educators accountable for results.
    b. Understanding which student learning needs present difficulties for educators.
    c. Demanding and supporting quality PD that improves teaching, leadership, and achievement.
    d. Allotting time and facilitating PD that will help educators address student learning problems.

57. Which of the following best defines equity?

    a. Providing all students with the same amount of resources and support
    b. Providing students with the resources and support that meet their individual needs
    c. Providing at-risk students with additional resources and support
    d. Providing accommodations for students who receive special education services

58. Which of the following is the best example of how school leaders can support teachers in developing their expertise and leadership skills?

    a. School leaders should increase teachers' workloads to give them opportunity to demonstrate responsibility.
    b. School leaders should develop all teachers in the same way to avoid building resentment among staff.
    c. School leaders must create safe environments for teachers' risk-taking and creative ideas.
    d. School leaders should limit how much authority to share with teachers to prevent diminishing their own authority.

59. A new student arrives in the country from Switzerland, speaks French, and is enrolled in XYZ High School. The only languages spoken at the school are English and Spanish. Which of the following actions should the school leader take in order to accommodate the needs of this student?

    a. Research Swiss culture.
    b. Pair the student with a peer to help the student get acclimated.
    c. Hire a translator to help communicate with the student.
    d. Meet with the student and their family to discuss their needs.

60. Which of the following strategies most accurately identifies the school leader's role in implementing professional development?

    a. Staff development is the sole responsibility of the school leader.
    b. A school leader should delegate the implementation of professional development to the administrative team.
    c. A school leader should leverage teacher leaders in the implementation of professional development.
    d. School leaders are directly responsible for implementing professional development but should utilize their administrative team and teacher leaders where appropriate.

61. Which of the following actions best demonstrates that a school leader is open to changing positions on an issue?

    a. The school leader lets staff vote on decisions.
    b. The school leader has an advisory committee made up of teachers, students, and community members.
    c. The school leader holds regular community meetings to provide updates on school activities.
    d. The school leader makes time to take phone calls from parents outside of school hours.

62. Which of the following informs how school leaders can incorporate diverse family and community aspirations and expectations into their educational decision-making and planning?

    a. Family aspirations for children vary markedly by culture.
    b. Ethnicity strongly influences family academic aspiration.
    c. Income affects family expectations more than race does.
    d. Studies find high family aspirations across demographics.

63. Which of the following most accurately reflects how school leaders can identify and decrease educational and institutional bias and discriminatory practices?

    a. Establishing anti-discrimination rules and identify a campus leader to enforce them.
    b. Establish an anti-discrimination policy and form a committee to find opportunities to learn about and promote other cultures.
    c. Hire a culturally diverse leadership team and have them speak to staff and students about their cultures.
    d. Include opportunities in the curriculum for students to learn about other cultures.

64. Staff morale at ABC Elementary school is very low and is impacting staff and student performance. Which of the following steps should the principal take first to repair staff morale?

    a. Host an all-staff pep rally to encourage everyone.
    b. Create a committee to advise the principal on how to repair staff morale.
    c. Buy gifts for the staff.
    d. Administer a survey to identify the causes of low morale.

65. Which of the following is true regarding how teacher evaluation standards should be designed?

    a. Teacher evaluations should reference clear instructional standards to prioritize student learning.
    b. Teacher evaluations should be conducted by school leaders with a single standardized measure.
    c. Teacher evaluations should be based on occasional observation and avoid critical commentaries.
    d. Teacher evaluations should play a minor part in important decisions about teacher employment.

66. XYZ school district requires a minimum number of professional development hours to be completed by teachers employed in the district annually. A high school principal notices that each year, teachers have difficulty meeting this expectation and look for last minute professional development opportunities at the end of the school year. What action might the principal take to address this issue?

    a. Personally deliver professional development sessions to staff monthly.
    b. Allocate more money in the budget to professional development.
    c. Monitor professional development activities more frequently throughout the school year.
    d. Provide incentives to teachers who complete all of their professional development activities at the beginning of the school year.

67. A middle school principal decides to select and train several lead teachers in the math department to conduct action research on campus. This decision is an example of which of the following strategies?

    a. Providing teachers with the opportunity to take appropriate risks for improving teaching and learning.
    b. Encouraging collaboration between teachers to support professional growth.
    c. Using data-driven decision making to improve student performance.
    d. Giving teachers voice in school decisions.

68. A school principal has reviewed assessment data and is concerned about the quality of learning on campus. Which of the following would be the best source of data for the principal to examine next?

    a. Student survey data
    b. Teacher survey data
    c. Classroom observation data
    d. Class size and student to teacher ratios

69. An assistant principal is reviewing a reading teacher's gradebook and notices that the students have very few grades entered for the marking period. The assistant principal is concerned and plans on meeting with the reading teacher. Which of the following questions is most important for the assistant principal to ask the teacher during this meeting?

    a. Are you aware of the grading policy in the faculty handbook?
    b. How many grades do you plan on assigning for the marking period?
    c. How do you document student mastery of objectives?
    d. Do you need help with grading assignments?

70. Which of the following laws dictates how student information can be used in an educational setting?

    a. HIPAA
    b. FERPA
    c. NCLB
    d. ESSA

Constructed Response

1. You are the principal of an 1800-student urban high school with a primarily African-American and Hispanic/Latino student population. The school has an active student newspaper with a much-beloved journalism teacher. Over the past several months, the student-staff have published several items of dubious origin that have caused controversy in the larger community. These items have typically had topics dealing with race relations. You have spoken to the journalism teacher after each incident about not allowing students to publish this type of questionable content. The newest issue of the student newspaper contains another such item. In 150-300 words, describe what you would do to address the situation.

2. You are the new principal of a 700-student elementary (K-5) school. The previous principal left the school in the midst of some controversy and there has been a significant turnover in teaching staff. In your first couple of weeks on the job, you notice a considerable amount of negativity among staff, in large part fomented by teachers who have been at the school for several years and have had multiple principals. In 300-600 words describe the strategies that you would use to address this negativity and change the culture of the school to a more positive tone and improve teacher and staff morale.

Answer Key and Explanations

Selected Response

1. A: In a culture of high expectations, staff and students strive towards high goals and excellence. A leader can create a culture of high expectations by setting campus goals above minimum standards. For example, if the expectation is that a school has at least a 90% attendance rate, the leader may set a goal of 95% for the school's attendance rate. Expecting students and staff to perform above minimum expectations creates a culture of high expectations.

2. A: Community resources used in the school must align with school programming. As a result, resources that will be used in the classroom must align with the curriculum. While it is important to consider a variety of other factors prior to incorporating community resources into the curriculum, it is imperative that the resources are aligned with the school vision and goals, which include the curriculum.

3. D: Teachers need opportunities to share their beliefs and ideas about teaching and learning with the school leader and with one another. Teachers must belief that they operate in an environment that allows them to be open and honest when examining their own beliefs and practices. Suggestion boxes and surveys are one-way communication tools that do not allow for peer discussion, although anonymity may help teachers feel comfortable giving honest feedback. Providing collaborative meeting time for teachers and meeting with them regularly gives teachers the opportunity to discuss their ideas with one another, but also gives them the opportunity to share their ideas with the school leader when they are comfortable.

4. C: School leaders should lead teachers to encourage solid student comprehension of concepts first, and only encourage students to use technology for enhancing their research and problem-solving skills after, not before (a), they understand concepts. They should not only lead but require teachers to instruct students in legal and ethical issues with accessing and using technology (b) and clearly differentiate with teachers between learning targets for student technology skills and learning targets for student thinking and content quality (d).

5. D: To help students prepare for their futures, high schools should design curricula relevant to students' lives, communities, and cultural milieus. This includes the career and technical education they will need for today's world, which public high schools must offer. School partnerships with colleges and universities best prepare students for higher education, while community-based and project-based learning best prepare students for employment.

6. B: The data suggests that the students need more rigorous instruction since they are performing well, but not demonstrating growth. Rigorous Standards-based curriculum can be delivered at an appropriate level of rigor so that students experience learning and demonstrate growth. Instructional delivery may include classes labeled as honors classes, pre-Advanced Placement, or Advanced Placement courses; however, classes do not have to be labeled in order for a teacher to increase the level of instruction in a classroom.

7. C: Diverse students are frequently overrepresented in special education due to inadequate educator knowledge and/or preparation for distinguishing such differences vs. true disabilities affecting learning and performance. School leaders address this inequity best by analyzing assessment instruments used to evaluate students for special education—which often require accommodations, modifications, or replacement with alternative assessments for diverse learners—rather than grade-level placement procedures because these students need instruction enabling them to perform at grade level, special education teaching strategies, or special curriculum and expectations, all of which are after the fact.

8. A: The school provides education and training to students that will make them employable in the community workforce. As a result, the school can supplement or adjust school programming to respond to the needs of the community, such as training students in particular employment fields that are experiencing a shortage within the community. Many schools, especially secondary schools, partner with their local community colleges and community organizations to identify employment trends in order to support the local community and increase the likelihood that graduates can obtain employment.

9. C: Providing ongoing feedback to teachers has the most significant impact on teacher performance. School leaders are responsible or evaluating teachers, providing feedback on evaluations, and assisting teachers with improving areas of weakness through coaching, mentoring, professional development and other strategies.

10. B: Although professional development (PD) must be job-embedded and school-based, it can occur even outside of the school building if teachers view it as part of their daily work duties and it emerges from and contributes to daily classroom practice. Teachers must be actively involved in the learning process for effective PD. PD should be student-centered, not teacher-centered because what teachers learn is to support student learning, not for teachers' own sake. Collaborative teacher problem-solving is both valuable and a PD guideline and addresses the issue of teacher isolation and as well as fosters professional and community respect.

11. C: Transparent decision-making is the act of making sure that the process, logic, and rationale used to make a decision are clear and available to be communicated to others. When decision-making is transparent, any critical information used to inform that decision is also readily available to others for review. This transparency allows others to understand how the decision was made.

12. D: A school leader should focus on improving all teaching on campus, even teaching that is already considered effective. This reinforces a culture of high expectations on campus and demonstrates to high-performing teachers that they are valued. When a school leader is committed to improving all instruction on campus, even instruction that is considered effective, all staff are encouraged to grow professionally for the benefit of students.

13. C: The principal has expressed a desire to engage in activities related to curriculum and instruction; therefore, assisting with lunch duty would not be an option. Analyzing data is a beneficial activity but is only indirectly related to curriculum and instruction. Similarly, tutoring students one time in isolation would not be beneficial use of the principal's time. Instead, the principal should engage in professional learning communities with teachers to discuss the implementation of curriculum and the results.

14. A: Before engaging any community resource, school leaders must consider whether it is compatible with the school's vision and mission. Some resources may have impact in the long-term rather than immediately and should not be discarded because effects will not be seen immediately. Additionally, as communities develop, new resources may be made available. Not all available resources will have a history of prior implementation but may prove beneficial for student learning. Similarly, as the school builds new partnerships, community resources may become available through new and emerging community relationships.

15. B: The new principal is aware that the teachers on campus are not happy; therefore, it is best to talk to a small group of teachers to understand what issues that they have. Sending a survey out is a good strategy, but not necessarily a first step as the data collected may not thoroughly describe the issues that the teachers have, especially if teachers do not feel that they can be honest on the survey. Also, an all-staff meeting can quickly get out of control if outspoken staff persons have unaddressed issues. Sending an email is impersonal and not an advisable first step.

16. A: Research studies have found the most effective implementations of school data use initiatives were most proactive, offering regular and expert system data use training of school leaders, leadership skills advice and coaching, and vigorous promotion. These got significantly better results even comparing districts using similar data systems, showing implementation was more important than the data system. Researchers observed that, although technology is necessary to support data initiatives, it alone is not the answer to school data use. Studies also found teams use data technology systems more quickly and productively than individual teachers.

17. C: The beginning of the school year is a critical time that can impact the success of the entire school year. Therefore, a leader should strive to have 100% of staff in place before school starts. Important trainings and professional development occur prior to the start of the year. A teacher who is hired later will miss these important trainings, which can impact their efficacy in the classroom and their ability to build relationships with the rest of the instructional team.

18. C: Analyzing videos of one's instructional practices is used in self-assessment and can also support reflection. Rather than relying on the observation feedback of a third party, the teacher can self-assess their proficiency in instructional delivery. Writing in a journal is used in reflection, not for self-assessment.

19. C: Cross-curricular instruction is the deliberate making of connections between various content areas so that students may apply their knowledge in more than one content area at a time. For example, students may examine the historical setting of a story in a reading class, utilize math strategies in a science class, or discuss geometric principles in an art class. Cross-curricular instruction is beneficial for students because it demonstrates the relevance of their content knowledge.

20. B: Research finds that school leader participation in PD is what determines teacher and school-wide participation in PD. School leaders set an example for teachers by actively engaging in the PD that teachers are expected to engage in. School leaders should have a vision for PD offerings but can empower teachers to choose PD offerings that meet their needs. School leaders can facilitate PD activities but should also allow teacher leaders to facilitate PD as well. School leaders should monitor implementation of PD but this activity is not directly related to being a role model for teachers.

21. A: Cultural diversity can affect academic achievement of students for a variety of reasons, including language barriers, cultural bias in curriculum, cultural bias in instructional practices and much more. If a particular demographic of students is not succeeding, the school leader must identify what the barriers to achievement are by talking with teachers, students, parents, and even community members. The school leader must then address those barriers by engaging diverse team members to meet the needs of all students on campus.

22. D: Researchers have found that, in more effective schools, novice teachers are assigned students with similar average achievement as students assigned to more experienced teachers; in other words, more effective schools and leaders assign classes more equitably to novice teachers than less effective schools do. More effective schools and leaders do not assign lower-achieving or higher-achieving students to novice teachers, nor do they assign them randomly relative to student achievement.

23. A: Tiered positive behavior support models have been found highly effective as school-wide classroom management systems because they incorporate not only prevention of behavior problems before they occur, but also interventions for existing or developing behavior problems. Also, by reducing the incidence of problem behaviors, these models provide *more* time for students to be engaged academically.

24. D: Researchers report a wide variety of school reform initiatives studied all commonly share one factor: leadership implicitly distributed among multiple individuals at schools. Studies also find that distributing leadership improves not only professional development of teachers (a) but also curriculum, assessment, and the development of professional communities in and among schools, led by teachers. Research finds the prodigious effort needed to make educational reform changes requires many good leaders, not just a few (b); broader-based capacity building requires distributing leadership more broadly, not limiting numbers of leaders (c).

25. D: When planning for differentiated instruction, teachers should utilize as much data as possible that can be useful in determining how students can best learn. Identification in special populations such as special education, English as second language, gifted and talented, and others are helpful when planning differentiated instruction but are not the only factors to be considered. Student interests, learning styles, formative and summative data, and other relevant data should all be considered when planning differentiated instruction.

26. D: Professional development sessions that take place over time, in contrast to single-session trainings are more likely to have an impact on teacher performance. Additionally, when a cohort of teachers participates in a training, there is opportunity for collaboration and collective accountability. There are benefits of providing individualized professional development opportunities for teachers; however, when these self-paced trainings are not time bound or accompanied by accountability measures, they are less likely to have a direct impact on current teacher performance.

27. C: Cooperative learning, the process of facilitating student collaboration develops social skills, teamwork, individual and collective responsibility, and group interdependence. The Socratic method is useful for facilitating student engagement, assessing student learning, and fostering critical thinking but is not useful for delivering instruction. Project-based learning is useful for active, hands-on learning experiences and does not require technology to be implemented effectively. Technology is a useful tool for delivering instruction, but is not required; technology is also effective when students utilize technology to engage in the learning process, making technology more student-centered.

28. A: The process of continuous improvement is the ongoing act of assessing performance and adjusting efforts in order to improve that performance. In order to implement a process of continuous improvement, there must be procedures of evaluation developed and implemented at regular checkpoints. Based on these regular evaluations, the leadership team can identify areas of improvement and initiate interventions and actions based on those identified areas. In schools, the regular evaluation of progress toward the campus vision and goals can be developed into a process of continuous improvement. However, campus leaders must focus on both the strengths and weaknesses of the campus in this process. Deficient areas can be improved to perform to standard, while areas performing at standard can be innovated for improvement.

29. C: The school culture can create a welcoming environment for new teachers, or it can repel them. When the school culture is positive, focused on students, and driven by excellence, teachers will want to be a part of that culture. They will be motivated by the positive culture and will recruit others to join the team. On the other hand, if the school culture is negative, then teachers and staff will likely have negative attitudes as well. Teachers will seek a way out of that school environment rather than encouraging others to join the team. This negative culture can negatively affect students' academic performance and behavior. If a potential teacher candidate observes a negative school culture, they may be unwilling to work at that campus.

30. B: Despite the students not showing growth on the district benchmark test, there is no evidence of the program's efficacy or inefficacy. First, the time period may be too short to determine if the program is effective. Secondly, it is unknown if the program was intended to have a direct impact on student performance measured by the benchmark exam. To determine the program's efficacy going forward, the leadership team must develop a plan for data collection and analysis at regular intervals. Only then can the leadership team determine the programs efficacy and whether the program should continue to be implemented on campus.

31. A: Mr. Smith's performance in the classroom does not excuse him from meeting other professional expectations. The assistant principal's response implies that Mr. Smith would be held accountable for his late arrival if he were not doing a good job in the classroom. It is unfair to allow Mr. Smith to arrive late without allowing other teachers to do the same. Integrity is most often applied to situations of morality, while justice is most often applied to situations in which the appropriateness of consequences is questioned. In this scenario, it is implied that the violation of policy for arrival time is based upon teaching performance, which would indicate that teachers who do not perform as well may be held to strict adherence to the policy. There is no discussion of morality or administered consequences in this scenario, only the unequal application of the policy.

32. A: Research shows that, among others, one reason schools should collaborate with their communities to provide mental health services is that schools are not suitable settings for clinical psychiatric care and similar services. When collaborating with communities, school staff must work not only with families and community service providers, but also with policymakers to coordinate and connect needed support processes. A cohesive and integrated mental health intervention continuum must address *both* severe student problems *and* universal student needs.

33. D: School leaders must maintain rigorous standards-based instruction across the campus. If students are not able to meet the standards, additional supports and interventions must be offered to students to address educational gaps. The math teacher cannot choose to lower the expectations or standards for students without permission and documentation according to local and state policies. The teacher does not demonstrate a need for training related to implementation of the curriculum, but the teacher must be directed to abide by the curriculum as written.

34. C: Staff growth though professional development is important. When identifying professional development for staff members, school leaders should consider school goals as well as individual goals of staff members. This will ensure that staff members are equipped to contribute to achieving school goals but also grow in areas that they have established personal goals.

35. B: Multiple research studies find that the most effective school leaders are better at identifying the teachers best and worst at increasing student performance among their existing faculty. However, researchers cannot determine whether the fact that effective school leaders also hire the best experienced teachers is more attributable to better leader ability in choosing teachers or to excellent teachers' attraction to schools with the best existing faculty quality. Researchers do

43

observe that school leaders cannot differentiate quality among average teachers as well as they can differentiate better from poorer teachers due to lesser contrast.

36. B: When students have satisfactory academic performance in class (reflected through items such as classroom assignments, teacher-created tests, and projects), but fail to meet satisfactory performance on standardized tests, that is an indication that what is taught in the classroom is not aligned with what is tested. This data trend shows that students are performing well based on the curriculum, but the curriculum does not adequately prepare students for what is assessed on the standardized test.

37. A: Traditionally, bus drivers are considered school support staff, typically under the district Transportation Department. They serve multiple school locations and are usually supervised by an employee in the Transportation Department. Custodians and cafeteria workers are often dedicated to one campus and may be supervised by the campus principal. Volunteers are unpaid and not officially school district employees, but are supervised by the campus principal to ensure compliance with policies and procedures. However, school districts may have differing organizational polices and supervision of campus personnel.

38. B: Traditional methods of assessment usually involve a standardized test with closed questions that require students to select an answer from several choices. Authentic assessment allows students to demonstrate mastery of content and objectives in different ways within the context of the subject matter. This may include project assessments, writing assessments, and performance assessment. The goal of authentic assessment is to provide students with the opportunity to authentically demonstrate that they have mastered the content.

39. C: Students designing digital storybooks is the best example of creating content using digital media. It is beneficial for students to access information using technology, such as visiting wiki pages. Students can also curate content that already exists, such as gathering photos from the web. However, creating content using digital media empowers students to use technology at the highest level of Bloom's taxonomy.

40. D: It would be most informative for the principal to ask a representative of the greatest variety of types of stakeholders to articulate the school vision to see if their responses are aligned or not. This will show how well he or she has communicated the vision to all involved rather than only comparing student and parent responses (a), only teacher and parent responses (b), or only different school staff members' responses (c).

41. B: According to researchers (Mitchell and Sackney, 1998), both reflection (i.e., considering their own practices) and conversation (i.e., discussing their and colleagues' practices) enable teachers to have awareness of their own and others' practices, evaluate them, and discover possible alternatives. These are cognitive processes. Affirmation of one another as professionals, and invitation into school decision-making both validate all staff members' contributions, acknowledge individual professional competencies, and thereby establish positive working relationships. These are affective processes.

42. B: In recent decades, environmental quality issues have emerged that affect school facility operations management. These include asbestos, radon, and other hazardous materials control; energy conservation; and improvement of water, indoor air quality, and acoustics, which may involve district support in hiring expert facility consultants. School leaders have government guidelines for food services (a); transportation (c) and custodial (d) services have existed longer than environmental awareness, have school policies and procedures in place, and are less likely to require expert consultation.

43. A: Each of the suggestions are viable options for the school leader to implement; however, the school leader needs to know why teachers leave or plan to leave in order to best address the problem. Seeking feedback from the teaching staff can help the school leader to focus resources on the most direct causes of teacher attrition. Once the causes are identified, the school leader can determine if the other suggestions are applicable.

44. B: Research from Stanford University (Grissom, Loeb, and Master, 2013) into effective school leader use of instructional time finds that improvements in student achievement are predicted by time spent on evaluation of teachers and/or curriculum, coaching teachers, and developing the school education program. It is *not* predicted in informal classroom walkthroughs, particularly in high schools. The investigators speculate this may be because school leaders frequently do not incorporate walkthroughs into broader strategies for school improvement.

45. C: Providing teachers with aggregated student data, even in regular intervals, will not likely improve teacher practice. School leaders must disaggregate data to help teachers identify the data that is reflective of their students and their instructional practice. Disaggregated data should also be analyzed in a collaborative process to help identify needs and generate solutions to address those needs.

46. A: A conflict of interest is a situation in which the school leader can obtain personal gain or harm from a decision they make as school leader. If it is determined that hiring the contractor who is related to the principal would bring the principal personal gain, then the situation could be deemed a conflict of interest.

47. D: Learning objectives are not what educators hope to accomplish, want to teach students, or what students expect teachers to impart to them. Instead, they are what educators expect their students to be able to do after they have instructed them in a content subject lesson, unit, or course. Experts observe that a common teacher error is to misinterpret learning objectives as things they plan to do during instruction instead of what they will expect students to do following instruction.

48. B: Experts believe that every school leader is motivated to conduct good teacher evaluations. However, they find one of the most important factors is whether school leaders make time to observe teachers regularly and frequently, even if only briefly each time. They emphasize that school leaders must evaluate teachers in a continuous process rather than a series of isolated events.

49. B: When teachers are given the power to choose their own professional development opportunities, they are given the opportunity to reflect on their own practice, identify their strengths and weaknesses, and participate in professional development that they believe is relevant. This contributes to building a risk-taking environment because teachers will be able to examine their own beliefs, values, and practices concerning teaching and learning and determine where they would like to improve.

50. C: According to principles of adult learning, adults learn best in more informal formats rather than how children learn by following a formal curriculum. They prefer guidance and choices rather than directive instruction. Both children and adults learn by doing, but active, hands-on participation is even more important for adult learning. Adults want to learn practical information they need and can use immediately in their work rather than theoretical concepts.

51. A: Student placement in courses should be based on relevant data. Automatically enrolling students in advanced placement courses without reviewing data could result in students being placed in classes that are too rigorous while students who were not previously enrolled could miss an opportunity to be placed in a challenging course. School leaders should monitor student performance data, ensure rigor and alignment of curriculum, and provide campus-wide opportunities for students when possible. In order to provide all students with preparation for and access to a challenging curriculum, students should have opportunities for an appropriate level of rigorous instruction based on their current academic performance.

52. A: Individual students have different learning styles, skills, strengths, and weaknesses, so it is important to administer multiple and varied assessments to assemble as comprehensive a picture as possible of each student's existing knowledge, new learning, and instructional needs. Multiple assessments are not used to keep students from forgetting. Summative assessments following instruction are not sufficient as they do not continuously assess student learning and progress, and they do not enable teachers to adjust ongoing instruction to be more effective as formative assessments made during instruction do.

53. A: Teachers and staff have more buy in when changes are made if they are part of the process. Creating a committee that does not include school leadership demonstrates the leader's willingness to give authority to the staff to promote change and a willingness to accept changes that are not generated by leadership. Suggestion boxes and town hall meetings allow staff to share ideas, but these ideas still must be vetted by the school leader as a gate keeper and may not fully address the school's current culture. Teacher engagement in the Shared Decision-Making Committee is vital for school success, but will not likely address a campus-wide perception of top-down leadership.

54. C: Adults learn in more productive ways when they know they have the right of choice whether to voluntarily learn or not, when they have choices among learning materials, when they are involved in planning the instruction they will be accessing, and when they are able to give instructors input about how their learning will be assessed.

55. A: Summative assessment is assessment that is used to evaluate student learning for mastery. Summative assessment usually occurs at the end of an instructional unit or a designated period of time, such as a grading period or school year. These assessments are aligned to objectives or standards and are usually high stakes, which means they may count for a significant grade or may determine a student's progress in their educational career. A summative assessment may be a midterm or final exam, a research project, a unit test, or a standardized exam. The results of summative assessments may determine a student's grade promotion or earning of course credit. Results from summative assessments may also determine a school's performance according to accountability standards. Summative assessment results are often used by school leaders for instructional planning and goal setting for the subsequent school year.

56. C: Parents and other community members must demand and support quality professional development (PD) that improves teaching, school leadership, and student achievement. School boards must hold educators accountable for results and provide policies clarifying that the purpose of PD is to enhance educator efficacy and thus student learning. Educators who organize and facilitate PD must understand which student learning needs they and their fellow educators have difficulty addressing. School system administrators must allot time and otherwise facilitate PD that will help educators address student learning problems.

57. B: All students are expected to meet the standards outlined by the state and federal government. School leaders are responsible for providing students with the instruction, resources, and support necessary to meet these standards. Equity refers to providing students with the resources and support that meet their individual needs. When leaders implement equity in schools, this may mean that some students receive more resources and support or different resources and support than others. This need may be due to a lack of educational opportunity, physical or intellectual disabilities, or other circumstances. Leaders must be aware of what students need so that the right resources and support can be used to support these students. All students will need resources and support to enrich their education, but practicing equity means that students will receive the appropriate amount of resources based on their identified needs.

58. C: To encourage teacher leadership, school leaders must create safe environments wherein teachers can take risks and think creatively. School leaders should share authority with teachers to assist them in developing leadership skills and demonstrate responsibility. Increasing a teacher's workload with work that is not directly related to increased responsibilities or to skill refinement is not an example of developing a teacher. Additionally, leaders must differentiate support for teachers based on the current performance, skill, and attitudes.

59. D: If possible, the school leader should communicate directly with the student and their family to learn about the student's academic, social, and emotional needs. Schools and school districts have policies and procedures for supporting students whose first language is not English so that these students can receive the support that they need to be academically successful.

60. D: The ultimate responsibility of developing and implementing professional development for teachers and staff belongs to the school leader. However, a school leader should leverage the knowledge and expertise of the administrative team and teacher leaders in this process. The school leader may provide the overall vision and goals and delegate some of the responsibilities relating to professional development to others while holding all parties accountable for meeting goals and aligning to the vision.

61. B: Creating an advisory committee and meeting with the committee regularly demonstrates that the leader is willing to hear other perspectives and opinions prior to making decisions. A school leader may believe one course of action is correct but then change their mind after receiving feedback from an advisory committee. A school leader can demonstrate a willingness to change by getting information from a variety of sources prior to making decisions.

62. D: Studies find that, regardless of culture, ethnicity, income, or race, diverse families overall tend to have very similar high aspirations and expectations for their children, care about their success similarly, and (within their means) share similar active involvement in their children's educations.

63. B: Establishing an anti-discrimination policy helps all staff and students to understand the regulations relating to bias and discrimination on campus. Describing what constitutes bias and discrimination makes it easier to identify violations on campus. Additionally, establishing a committee that is focused on cultural awareness and inclusion can help to decrease educational and institutional bias and discriminatory practices. Establishing and enforcing rules as limited efficacy if there is limited understanding of the rationale behind the rules. Having a culturally diverse staff is beneficially, but persons of underrepresented cultures should not be required to teach others about their cultures if they do not choose to. It is beneficial to include opportunities for students to learn about other cultures in the classroom, however this strategy does help to identify bias and discriminatory practices on campus.

64. D: The first step that a principal must take is to determine the causes of the low morale. Implementing solutions without understanding the causes may lead to wasted time and resources if the solutions do not address the perceived problems. The principal should collect data to identify the issues that staff may have on campus and then develop appropriate solutions.

65. A: According to the New Teacher Project (2011), design standards for effective teacher evaluation systems include evaluating teachers a minimum of yearly, using multiple levels (four or five) for rating teachers, basing evaluations on clear instructional excellence standards prioritizing student learning, using multiple performance measures emphasizing teacher impact on student academic progress, making frequent observations and giving critical and/or constructive feedback, and making evaluation outcomes significant by using them as a major factor in important teacher employment decisions.

66. C: The goal of professional development is to foster continuous improvement of teaching and learning. Professional development has limited applicability if it is all conducted at the beginning of the school year or at the end of the school year. The best action that the principal can take is to monitor professional development at regular intervals throughout the school year and to encourage teachers to take advantage of timely professional development that can impact their practice during the school year.

67. A: Supporting teachers in conducting action research on campus is an example of giving them opportunities to take risks for improving teaching and learning. Action research allows the teacher to identify the area of improvement and hypothesize which actions or strategies may lead to improving the identified area. Action research allows teachers to problem solve using solutions that they have developed which gives them the opportunity to take risks.

68. C: The school leader observing classroom instruction also provides opportunities to observe students in the learning process. Classroom observations can provide valuable information about instructional delivery, teacher quality, and student performance. Reviewing classroom observation data in conjunction with student academic performance data can provide the school leader with a more well-rounded understanding of the quality of learning on campus.

69. C: Grades should reflect student mastery of objectives. The assistant principal needs to know if the reading teacher is assessing students properly to assign grades and if so, determine why measurements of student progress and mastery are not entered into the gradebook in a timely manner.

70. B: FERPA stands for the Family Educational Rights and Privacy Act. It is a federal law that protects student information and education records.